Czerny for the Developing Pianist

Selections from *The Little Pianist, Opus 823*

Margaret Otwell, Editor

Carol Klose and Jennifer Linn, Assistant Editors

About This Edition

The twenty-nine etudes in this book are taken from Carl Czerny's *The Little Pianist, Opus 823*. These engaging etudes are comparable to their famous "older brothers," the studies found in *The Art of Finger Dexterity*, but are written for students at an earlier stage of study. They encompass a wealth of technical and music instruction from this master teacher of the Classical period, indeed, the world's first, great piano pedagogue. The etudes focus on developing both technical and music skills, providing an excellent stylistic and technical resource for the late-elementary to early-intermediate pianist.

Some editorial changes were made to the original G. Schirmer engravings:

- Adjustments were made to slurs and articulation in several etudes. These changes were made by the editors to elicit a stylistically appropriate and consistent interpretation.

- In some etudes, dynamic symbols were added to guide the student's interpretation.

- Fingering suggestions have been provided throughout the book by the editors.

- Metronome indications have been added at the beginning of each etude for both a practice and a performance tempo ($\quarternote = 112$/$\quarternote = 160$). These correspond directly to the orchestrations that are available in the book/audio version.

- It is equally important to state that no notes have been changed, nor has the character or tempo of any etude been altered in any way.

We have also added these original features:

- Preceding each etude or group of etudes is a worksheet divided into three sections: **Practice Tips**, **Quick Quiz**, and **Creative Corner**. These worksheets will help students focus on the important technical features in each etude, apply practical music theory to their study of the music, and vary the etudes in creative ways.

- Orchestrated accompaniments are available for each etude.

ISBN 978-0-634-05772-4

G. SCHIRMER, Inc.

DISTRIBUTED BY

Visit Hal Leonard Online at
www.halleonard.com

World headquarters, contact:
Hal Leonard
7777 West Bluemound Road
Milwaukee, WI 53213
Email: info@halleonard.com

In Europe, contact:
Hal Leonard Europe Limited
1 Red Place
London, W1K 6PL
Email: info@halleonardeurope.com

In Australia, contact:
Hal Leonard Australia Pty. Ltd.
4 Lentara Court
Cheltenham, Victoria, 3192 Australia
Email: info@halleonard.com.au

Table of Contents

About the Composer

Viennese pianist and composer Carl Czerny has influenced and shaped the world's pianists for more than two centuries. Yet he is not remembered for his brilliant performances, nor for his more than 1000 compositions. Instead, he is remembered for his tireless work in preserving Beethoven's legacy and for the thousands of exacting, technique-building exercises he wrote for pianists, many of which are still in use today.

Czerny began the most significant musical relationship of his life in 1801, when at the age of 10 he began studying with Beethoven. Although the young pianist had made his concert debut a year earlier, he found in Beethoven a tremendously illuminating mentor. The two formed a close friendship that endured until Beethoven's death in 1827. In 1842, Czerny wrote in *Erinnerungen aus meinem Leben* (Memories from My Life): "Beethoven had me concentrate exclusively on scales in all the keys and showed me the only correct position of the hands and fingers (unknown as yet to most players at that time), and especially the use of the thumb – rules whose value I came to appreciate only much later." Beethoven also stressed the importance of *legato* playing, which many players felt was impossible on the pianoforte that was in use at the time.

Carl Czerny

Beginning his own long teaching career at age 15, Czerny used Beethoven's works and ideas as the basis of his approach. He saw himself as the person best equipped to pass Beethoven's legacy to another generation of musicians. He taught many prominent figures, including the great pianist and composer Franz Liszt and Beethoven's beloved nephew, Karl. Beethoven's music became Czerny's passion. He arranged private concerts devoted to Beethoven's works, some of which Beethoven is known to have attended. He was able to play all of Beethoven's piano works from memory. In a day when concerts were an expensive luxury for many, and recording technology capable of reproducing orchestral sound was still a century away, Czerny brought some of Beethoven's orchestral and chamber music to the masses through his two- and four-hand piano transcriptions. Beethoven approved and supervised some of these transcriptions. Czerny also compiled and edited all of Beethoven's piano pieces.

Czerny had the good fortune to have been born into an age ripe for his special skills. Chopin (1810-1849) and Liszt (1811-1886) were bringing their fiery brand of virtuosity to huge audiences all over Europe during Czerny's lifetime. At the same time, the piano itself was undergoing changes in both design, construction, and manufacturing, leading to the availability of a more refined, responsive instrument. The perfection of the hammer system within the instrument allowed players to execute faster passage work and repeated notes than they could on earlier instruments. The smoother action and addition of pedals expanded the instrument's ability to make long *legato* phrases. Mass-production techniques were beginning to make pianos more affordable to the general public, increasing the demand for teachers and method materials. The time was right for Czerny's pedagogy, making him a wealthy man by the time of his death in 1857. Although Czerny wrote symphonies, chamber pieces, sacred music, and numerous piano pieces, it was his many volumes of exercises and studies, covering scales, embellishments, *legato* and *staccato* playing, octaves, and even improvement of the left hand and studies for small hands, that forever raised the level of technical fluency expected of professional and amateur players alike.

But this pillar of the piano world led a lonely life. Born in 1791, he was an only child and was in his own words, "under my parents' constant supervision" and "carefully isolated from other children." He lived with his parents in his adulthood, until his mother died in 1827, and his father in 1832. He never married, living alone after his parents' deaths for the rest of his life. Although his early performances won him praise from Viennese critics, Czerny never pursued a concert career. A concert tour was planned in 1805, complete with a testimonial from Beethoven, but was canceled due to political unrest. Czerny explained his choice to teach and compose rather than perform, saying that he felt his playing lacked certain elements essential to a concert artist. The truth more likely lay in his fragile health and retiring nature, both of which were poorly suited to a concert career. But the work of this quiet man, who spent his life in Vienna, can be heard throughout the world today.

– *Elaine Schmidt*

Theory Basics

In the *Quick Quiz* section of each worksheet, you will be asked to identify intervals, triads, and chord inversions. The reference chart below defines these important concepts.

Intervals

An *interval* is the distance from one key to another key on the keyboard, and from one note to another note on the staff.

Intervals are counted beginning with the first note indicated, and ending with the second note. For example, in the chart below, the distance from C to E is a 3rd because you have counted the notes C-D-E.

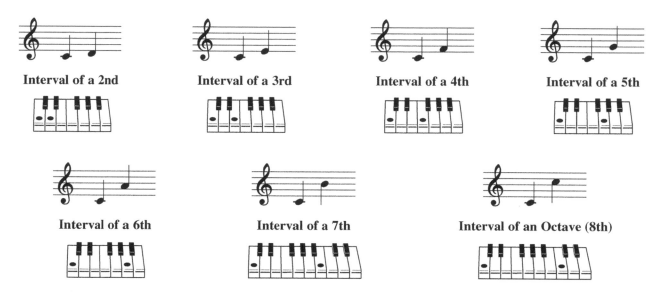

Triads and Inversions

A triad can have three positions: *root position*, *first inversion*, or *second inversion*. The lowest note of the chord determines the position of the chord.

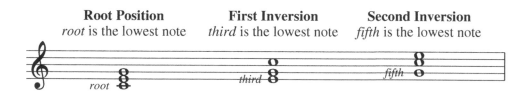

When a chord is inverted, the lowest note and the intervals that form the chord change, but the note names remain the same.

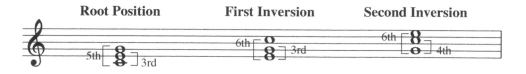

Chords of the Key

Chords built on the 1st, 4th, and 5th degrees of the scale are called *primary triads*. These triads are identified by the Roman numerals **I**, **IV**, and **V** or **V7**.

General Practice Tips

- Prepare for each new etude by doing the activities suggested on the study page with your teacher.

- Keep a steady pulse from beginning to end, using a metronome as you practice. Begin with your metronome set at the *practice* tempo, indicated by the first number in the metronome indication found at the beginning of each etude. When you can play the etude comfortably at that speed, steadily increase your practice tempo by setting your metronome at a gradually faster pace ($\quarternote$ = 72, 84 etc.) with the *performance* tempo, indicated by the second metronome number, as your goal.

- A good hand position will help you to play with maximum ease. Curve your fingers and support them with a relaxed, rounded hand position and a level wrist and forearm.

- Balance the weight of your hand and arm over each finger as you play, moving smoothly from finger to finger.

- Play with a full, rich sound, even in *piano* passages. Let your ear act as a teacher for your fingers. Listening carefully to the sound that you make will help you create a rich and varied sound, enhancing the musicality of your performance.

- Timing is everything! Be certain that you know *when* and *which* left-hand notes must be played at exactly the same time as corresponding right-hand notes.

- When you can play the entire etude confidently at the performance tempo, you are ready to work on the suggestions in *Creative Corner*.

- In addition to the specific variations suggested for each etude in *Creative Corner*, use your own imagination to improvise other variations and to compose new pieces from the materials in the original etude.

A Note to the Teacher

The practice and performance suggestions in this edition reflect a contemporary approach to piano technique that emphasizes interdependence of the fingers, hand, wrist and arm. Czerny's brief etudes are excellent choices for the development of agility, rhythmic precision, good aural skills, and musical style. We recommend that upon mastering this volume, students progress to the original *G. Schirmer* edition of *The Little Pianist, Op. 823* (HL50252390) to further develop their technique and continue to explore these classic studies by Carl Czerny.

Margaret Otwell

Etudes 1, 2, 3, and 4

Practice Tips

- In *Etudes 1* through *4*, the notes lie mainly within the C Major five-finger pattern. To become used to the fingering in these etudes, first practice *silently* on your lap, or on the closed lid of the piano.
- Play with a full, rich tone and listen carefully for the R.H. and L.H. notes to sound at exactly the same time.
- Keep your wrist flexible and the weight of your arm balanced over each note as you play.
- In *Etudes 1* and *2*, relax your wrist and arm as you hold the second beat of each half note.

  (Etude 1, m.1)

  R.H. 2

  1 - 2 - 3 - 4
  Play Hold Play Hold
       and   and
       relax   relax

- In *Etude 3*, play the R.H. notes *non legato*. Feel the quarter notes in groups of 2's, placing less arm weight on the repeated note in each group.

Quick Quiz

1. In *Etude 1*, measures 1-4, the interval between the R.H. and L.H. notes is a 10th (an octave plus a 3rd). What is the interval between the R.H. and L.H. notes in measures 5-7? _____
2. In *Etude 2*, compare measures 1-2 and 5-6. Circle the note that is different.
3. Compare the R.H. parts in *Etudes 2* and *3*. How are they similar?
4. What major triad is outlined in the first two measures of *Etudes 2, 3,* and *4*? _____

Creative Corner

- Make up a new L.H. accompaniment for *Etudes 2* and *3* by playing blocked **I** and **V7** chords in C Major, as shown in this example.

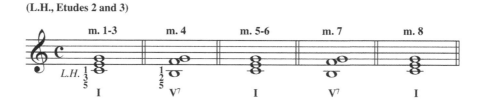

(L.H., Etudes 2 and 3)

- Draw a vertical line down the length of the entire page, along the bar line between measure 4 and 5 of each etude. This line will divide each etude in half (m. 1-4, and m. 5-8). Mix and match these four-measure groups to create a new piece. For example, combine the first half of *Etude 1* with the last half of *Etude 3*. How many 'new' pieces can you play?
- Add *staccatos* to the quarter notes in *Etudes 3* and *4*, and play the two etudes back to back without pausing. Name your new piece.
- Transpose *Etude 4* to G Major.

1.

2.

3.

4.

Etudes 5, 6, and 7

Practice Tips – Etude 5

- Your left hand must extend at times to reach harmonic intervals larger than a 5th. Play with a flexible wrist and curved fingers, and distribute the weight of your hand evenly over the notes of each interval or chord.
- Play the L.H. intervals and chords *legato*, keeping your fingers close to the keys as you play.
- Connect all R.H. notes within each slur to the very end. Focus on this skill in the warm-up below.

Practice Tips – Etude 6

- Play each slur with a single, drop/lift motion of the arm and wrist. In measures with three repeated notes, bounce your wrist gently on each note.

Practice Tips – Etude 7

- The R.H. and L.H. do not always play *legato* at the same time. Practice slowly at first, making sure that each hand plays *legato* through the end of each slur.
- As you play the L.H. part in *Etude 7*, measures 1-4, keep your hand gently arched and support finger 5 with the large muscle on the outside of your hand. The 5th finger gives a natural pulse to each pattern. Be careful not to accent the thumb notes.

Quick Quiz

1. In *Etude 5*, play measures 1-2, 5-6, and 13-14. Which of these phrases sounds different? Why?
2. In *Etude 7*, how many measures are made up of chord tones belonging to the **V7** (G7) chord in C Major? (Be sure to check both the R.H. and L.H. notes in each measure.) _____

Creative Corner

- Make up your own variation of *Etude 6*. Play the R.H. part as written, and create a new L.H. part by playing a mirror image of the R.H. part. Match the fingering throughout. Add crisp *staccatos* on all repeated notes. Listen to the mood of your new etude and give it a fitting title.

5.

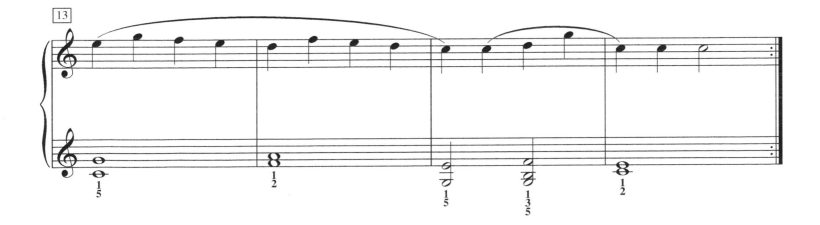

11

6.

(= 100/160)

7.

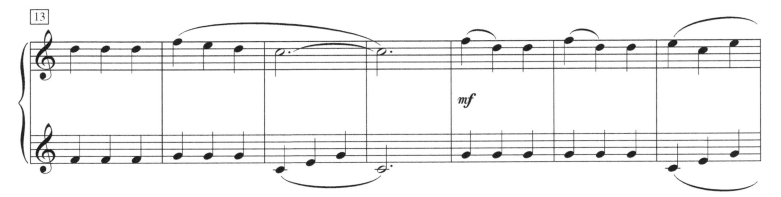

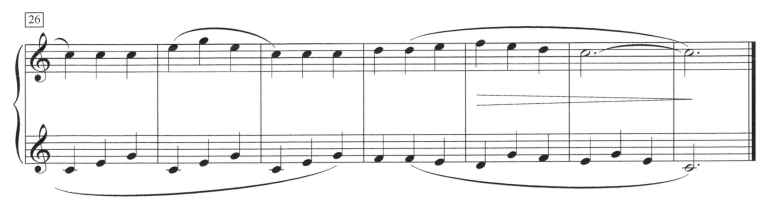

Etudes 8, 9, and 10

Practice Tips

- When playing continuous quarter notes in 3/4 time, group them in 3's with a natural pulse on beat one. Use a drop/lift motion of the arm and wrist for each group. Use this technique in the R.H. of *Etude 8*, and in the L.H. of *Etudes 9* and *10*.

Practice Tips – Etude 8

- When one hand has a melody and the other has an accompaniment, it is important to bring out the melodic line and keep the accompaniment at a lower dynamic level. Play the L.H. accompaniment softly, but with a good sound and secure touch, keeping your wrist flexible and your arm relaxed.

- The warm-up to the right will help you shift with ease between the intervals in the L.H. accompaniment. Practice transferring your arm weight smoothly between L.H. fingers 1-3 and 2-5.

Practice Tips – Etude 9 and 10

- First practice the L.H. alone, blocking the chords in each measure to become familiar with the harmonic patterns. Then practice the R.H. melody with L.H. blocked chords before playing the etude as written.
- Play the L.H. part *legato* throughout, without overlapping the sound.
- Keep a level hand and flexible wrist as you play, and avoid tipping your hand over to one side as you play finger 5.
- Play the R.H. with a light, lilting touch. Play in four-measure phrases, keeping the music moving steadily through each phrase to the end.

Quick Quiz

1. *Etude 9* is in what key? _____
2. Find and play all the L.H. measures that are made up of the **V** or **V7** chords in that key.
3. In *Etude 10*, name the chord outlined in the L.H., measure 21. _____
4. Is that chord in root position, first inversion, or second inversion? _____

Creative Corner

- Make up your own variation of *Etude 8* by changing the L.H. intervals from harmonic to melodic, repeating the upper note on beat 3, as shown below.

- Make a variation of *Etude 9* by crossing the R.H. over the L.H. and playing the R.H. melody two octaves lower than written. Play the L.H. as written.

8.

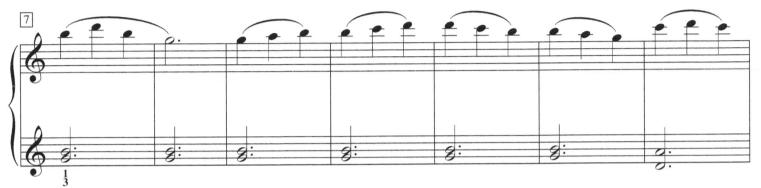

9.

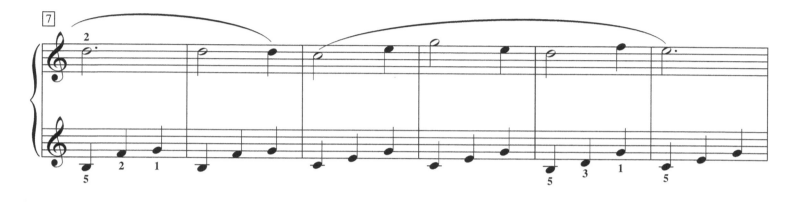

10.

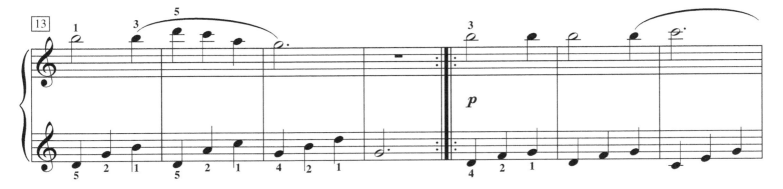

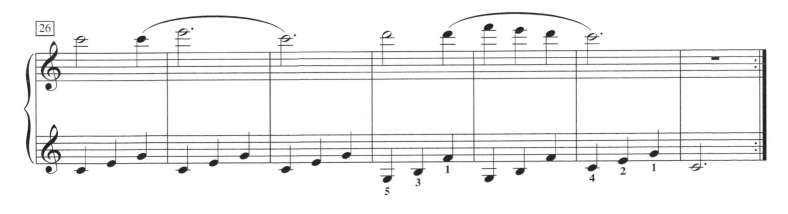

Etudes 11, 12, and 13

Practice Tips

- In each of these etudes, focus on bringing out the R.H. melody more than the L.H. accompaniment. Practice this first by fingering the L.H. part *silently* on the surface of the keys, while actually playing the R.H. notes, using full arm weight.

Practice Tips – Etude 11

- There are four phrase groups in the R.H. melody. Each group is four measures long. As you practice, listen to the rise and fall of the melody line and shape each group with ⟍⟋ and ⟋⟍ .
- The L.H. accompaniment pattern in measure 1 is known as an *Alberti Bass*, named for the Italian classical-period composer, Domenico Alberti (1710-1740), who used it frequently. For this and similar patterns, keep your hand gently arched, being careful not to collapse finger 5. Give a natural pulse to the first note, decreasing the sound on the other three notes.

Practice Tips – Etude 12

- In measure 1, circle the L.H. eighth notes on beats 1, 2, 3, 4, and also on beat 1, measure 2. These notes form a 'duet' with the R.H. melody notes above them. Listen to this duet as you play the following warm-up, and when you play the etude as written.

(Etude 12)

Practice Tips – Etude 12 and 13

- Practice the L.H. eighth notes slowly at first. Keep your arm weight balanced over fingers 5-4-3 so your thumb can play lightly throughout. Think of each L.H. measure in two large groups, with a natural pulse on beats 1 and 3.

Practice Tips – Etude 13

- Coordinate the *legato* and *staccato* touches in both hands by remembering to pass the sounds of the *legato* notes from finger to finger, while using light wrist bounces to play the R.H. *staccato* notes.

Quick Quiz

1. *Etude 11* is in what key? _____
2. In *Etude 12*, play beat 1 of each of the following measures and name the interval between the R.H. and L.H. notes: measure 1 _____; measure 5 _____; measure 9 _____; measure 13 _____.

Creative Corner

- Change the key of *Etude 11* from G Major to its minor mode, G minor. Remember to play all the B's as B-flats. Listen to the new mood created by the minor sound. Experiment with slow and fast tempos, as well as *f* and *p* dynamics.
- Give *Etude 13* a 'jazz' feel by playing the L.H. in 'swing eighths.' (♫ = ♩♪)
- By changing the *register* (highness or lowness) of a piece, you can give it an entirely different character. Play *Etude 13* with the L.H. part an octave higher. What title would you give this new version?

11.

12.

13.

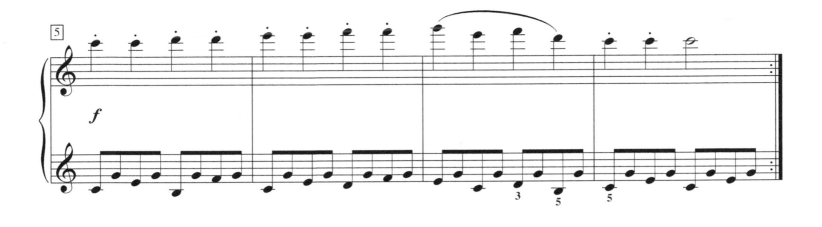

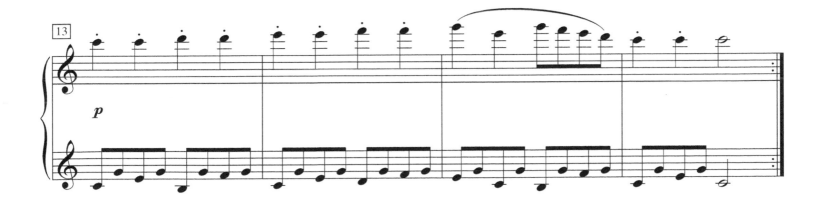

Etude 14

Practice Tips

- A combination of R.H. slurs and *staccatos* gives *Etude 14* a dance-like character. Play each slur with a single, drop/lift motion of your wrist and arm.
- Play the R.H. *staccato* notes with a lightly bouncing wrist. In measure 3, make the repeated notes sound slightly longer than the *staccato* notes.
- Play the R.H. notes in measures 11 and 12 in two groups, giving a natural pulse to beats 1 and 3. Be careful to release your hand at the end of each slur.
- As you play the L.H. part, keep your arm weight balanced over fingers 1 and 2 so finger 5 can play lightly throughout. Be careful to keep your hand from tipping over to one side as you play finger 5.

Quick Quiz

1. In the excerpt below, name the chord outlined in the first measure. _____
2. Is that chord in root position, first inversion, or second inversion? _____
3. Name the chord outlined in the second measure. _____
4. Name the common tone between the two chords in the excerpt. _____

(Etude 14, m. 2-3)

5. Notes that move by step between two chord tones are called *passing tones*. Circle the passing tones in the R.H. part, measure 1 and measure 9.

Creative Corner

- Improvise a new R.H. melody for this etude, using notes in the G Major 5-finger pattern and the L.H. accompaniment as written. Include chord tones and passing tones, letting your ear guide you.
- Transpose this etude to C Major. The L.H. chords are shown below:

(Etude 14)

14.

23

Etude 15

Practice Tips

- This is the first etude in 6/8 meter in this book. Pieces in 6/8 meter are usually felt in two pulses per measure.

- To feel the natural pulse, conduct the beats in 'two' with full-arm motions, as you count all six beats aloud.

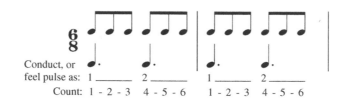

- In the L.H. part, play each group of three notes with a 'down-up' motion of the wrist. Play with a natural pulse on beats 1 and 4 for a musical, dance-like accompaniment.

(Etude 15)

- Remember to play the two-note slurs in the R.H. part, measures 4 and 8 with a gentle drop/lift motion and a slight *diminuendo*.

- The R.H. and L.H. do not always play *legato* at the same time. Make sure that the R.H. plays *legato* through the end of each slur, while the L.H. maintains the 'down-up' motion. Focus on this skill by actually playing the R.H. part on the keyboard while *silently* fingering the L.H. part on your knee. Listen carefully for a smooth *legato* sound throughout each slur.

Quick Quiz

1. *Question phrases* often end on the dominant (fifth scale degree) of the melody, and *answer phrases* usually end on the tonic (first scale degree). In *Etude 15*, these question and answer phrases are all four measures long.
   How many question phrases are there in this etude? _____ measure(s)_____
   How many answer phrases? _____ measure(s)_____

2. Name the R.H. chord outlined in the last three beats in measure 1. _____
   Is this chord in root position, first inversion, or second inversion? _____

3. Name the R.H. chord outlined in the last three beats in measure 13. _____
   Is this chord in root position, first inversion, or second inversion? _____

Creative Corner

- Make up a new version of this etude by changing the L.H. accompaniment to a broken-chord pattern, as shown to the right.

- Give your new piece a title.

(Etude 15)

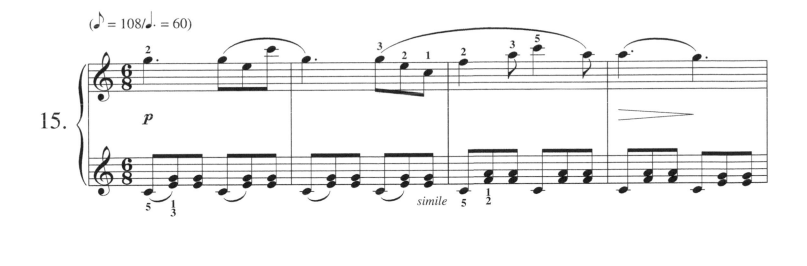

15.

Etude 16

Practice Tips

- First practice the L.H. alone, blocking the chords in each measure to become familiar with the harmonic patterns. Then practice the R.H. melody with L.H. blocked chords before playing the etude as written.

- As you play the triplet figures in the L.H., be careful not to tip your hand over to one side.

- Keep the thumb notes light and play with a slight *diminuendo* to the thumb.

- Keep the L.H. triplets moving at a very steady pace with an even, light sound throughout.

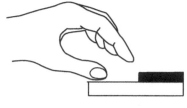

Keep a good arch.

- Focus on bringing out the R.H. melody more than the L.H. accompaniment. Practice this by fingering the L.H. part *silently* on the surface of the keys, while actually playing the R.H. melody using full arm weight.

Quick Quiz

In the excerpt below, name the chords of the key in each measure, writing **I**, **IV**, **V**, or **V7** in the blanks.

(Etude 16, m. 1-8)

Creative Corner

- Play the R.H. part one octave higher on the repeat of each section. Is it *more* or *less* difficult to project the melody when playing *8va*? Why?

- A piece in C Major is easy to transpose to C♯ Major – the key that uses all seven sharps in its key signature. Simply read the same notes, but play them all as sharps. Don't forget the white-key sharps E♯ and B♯. The fingering will remain the same. (If you are using the General MIDI accompaniment disk for this book, transpose the track up one half-step.)

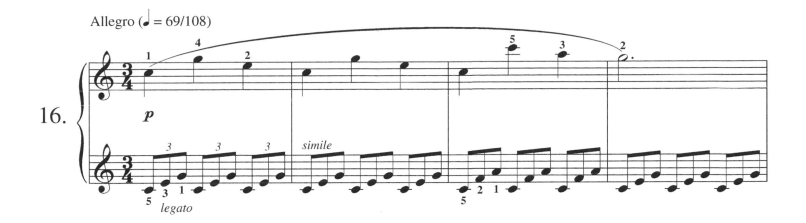

16.

Allegro (♩ = 69/108)

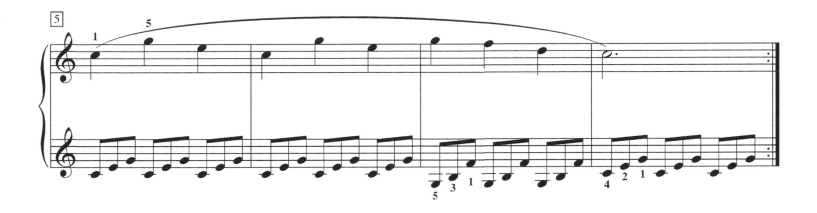

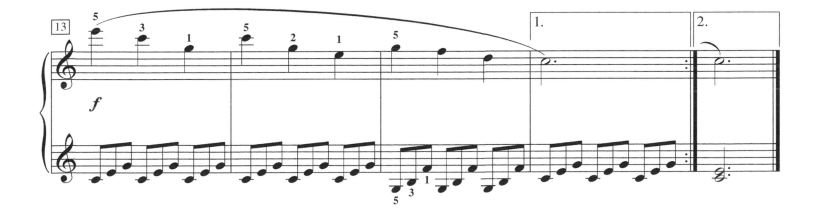

Etudes 17, 18, and 19

Practice Tips

- These three etudes focus on playing double thirds with either a *legato* or *staccato* touch.

Practice Tips – Etudes 17 and 18

- When moving between *legato* double thirds that share a common note, it is necessary to release the common note while holding the note that can be connected. This creates the illusion of a true *legato* sound. Practice this skill in the warm-ups below, keeping your fingers as close as possible to the surface of the keys at all times.

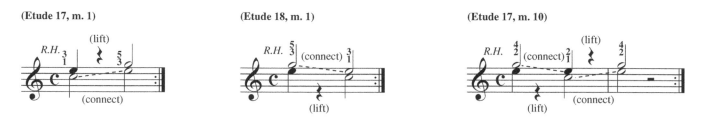

Apply this skill wherever double thirds share a common tone in *Etudes 17* and *18*.

- Use this same technique when playing double thirds that require a finger crossover. Focus on this skill in the warm-up to the right.

  Apply this skill in *Etude 17*, R.H. measure 7-8.

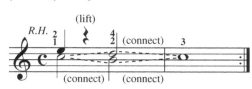

Practice Tips – Etude 19

- In measures 1 and 2, the R.H. notes cover the distance of an octave. To play with ease, keep your wrist flexible and your arms and shoulders relaxed, centering your arm weight over each finger that plays. Let your hand and arm follow your fingers as you play.

Quick Quiz

Play the R.H. part, measure 1, of *Etude 17* and circle the diagram below which best describes the wrist motion used.

Creative Corner

- Change the key of *Etude 19* from C Major to its minor mode, C minor. Remember to play all the E-naturals as E-flats and all the A-naturals as A-flats. Listen to the new mood created by the minor sound. Experiment with slow and fast tempos, as well as contrasting dynamics.

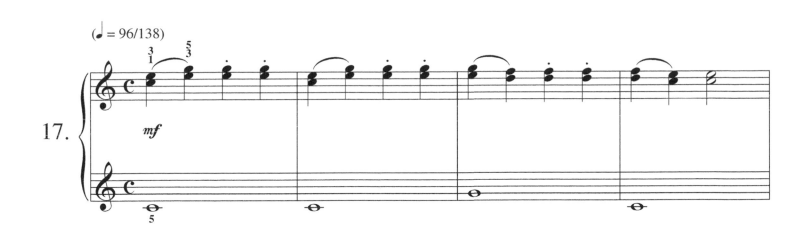

17.

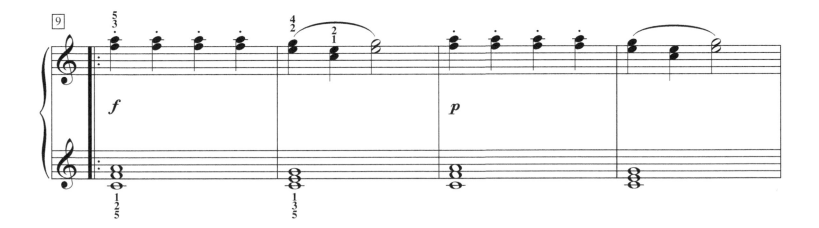

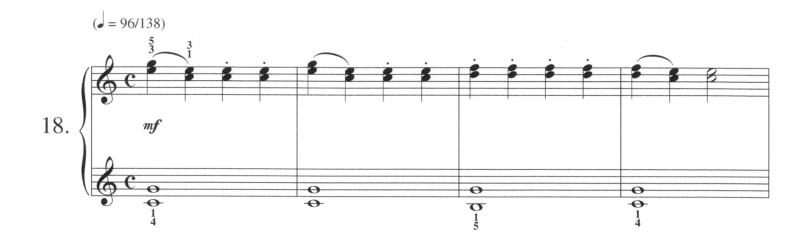

18.

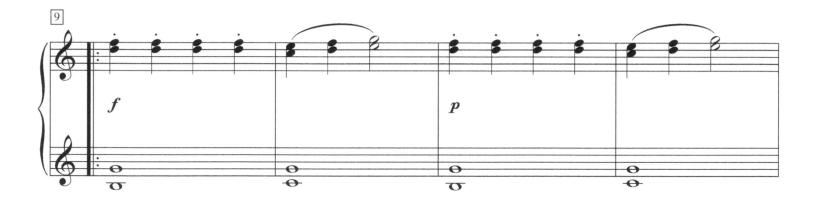

19.

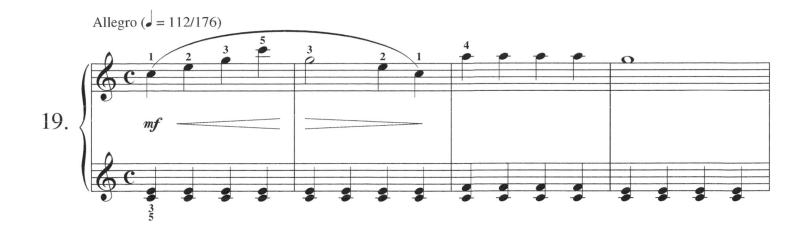

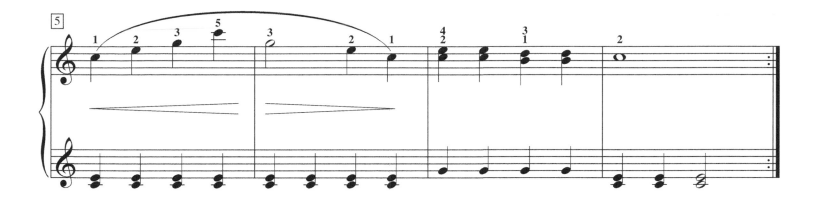

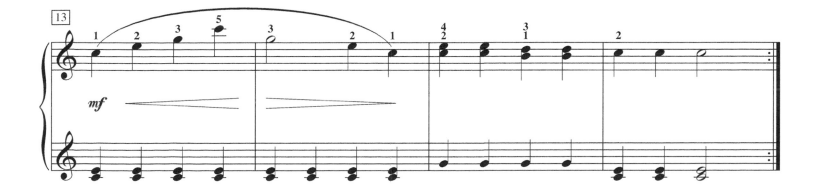

Etudes 20, 21, and 22

Practice Tips

- In each of these etudes, the L.H. must hold one note on the downbeat while playing additional notes on the remaining beats in the measure.
- Center the weight of your hand over the held note, supporting finger 5 with the large muscle of your hand so that it does not collapse. Play the repeated notes in each measure with a flexible wrist and a light touch. Practice this technique in the warm-ups below.

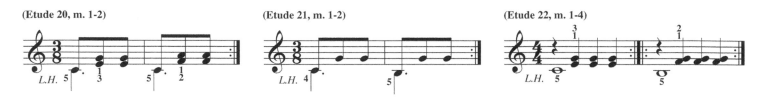

Practice Tips – Etude 21

- Keep the shape of the 6ths in your R.H., playing each one with a flexible motion of the wrist, tapping the keys lightly with your fingertips. Feel the distance from one 6th to the next without looking at the keys. Practice this skill in the warm-up below.

Quick Quiz

1. The L.H. pattern found in *Etude 22*, measure 17-23, is another example of *Alberti Bass* (described earlier on page 18). Name three composers from the Classical era who used this pattern in their compositions.

   _____   _____   _____

2. In the excerpt below, fill in each blank with the name of the chord outlined in each measure.
   Add **I**, **V**, or **V7** in the second blank in each measure to show the chord's function in the key.

Creative Corner

- Add ⟍ and ⟋ to each four-measure phrase of *Etude 20*.
- Improvise a new R.H. melody for *Etude 22*, using the C Major scale tones. Play the L.H. accompaniment as written. Include chord tones and passing tones, letting your ear guide you.

20.

Allegretto (♪ = 112/♩. = 60)

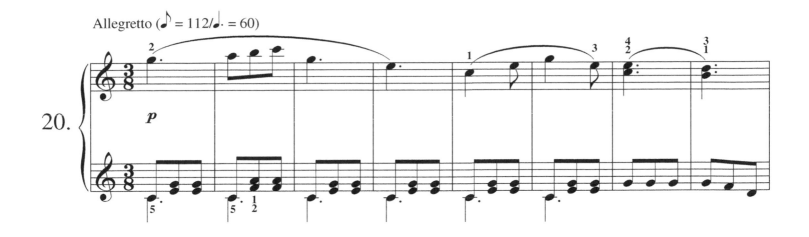

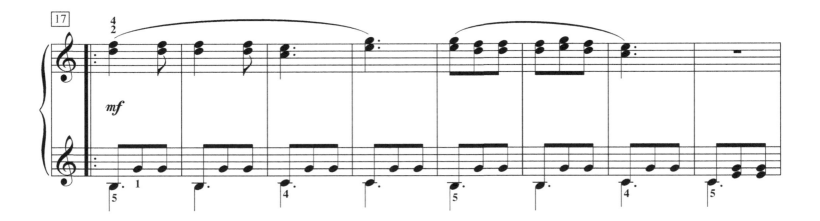

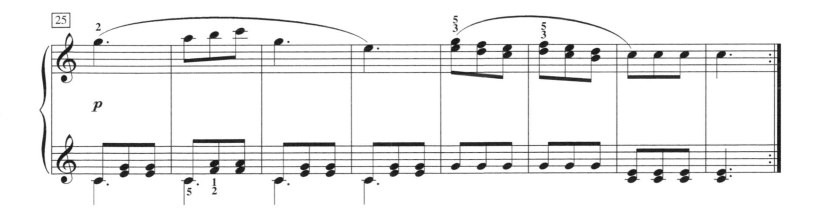

33

Vivace (♪ = 108/♩. = 69)

21.

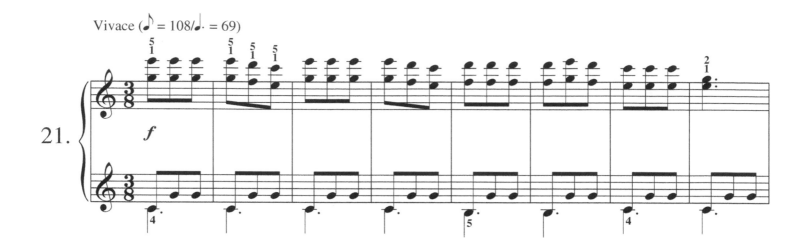

34

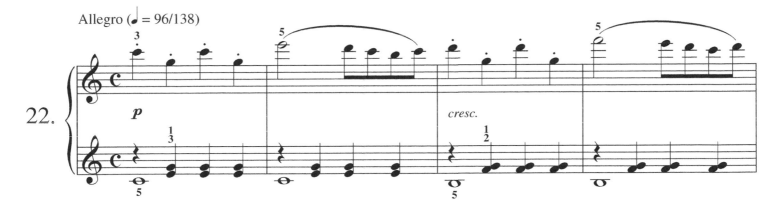

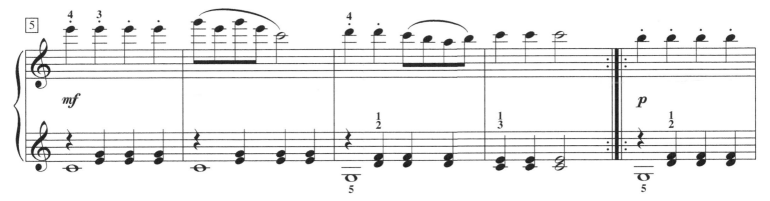

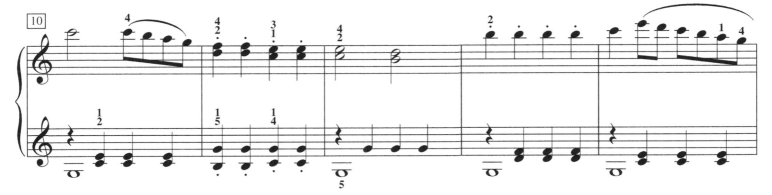

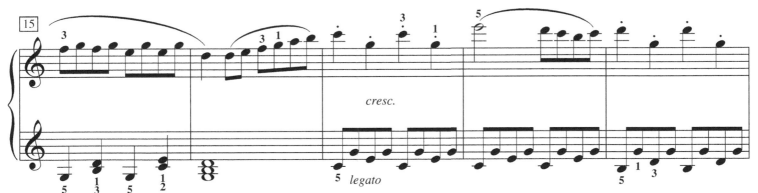

Etude 23

Practice Tips

- To bring out the R.H. melody, play the L.H. at a softer dynamic level.
- Play all the L.H. thumb notes *very* lightly. Focus on this skill in the warm-up below, with the thumb *silently* touching each note marked with an "X".

- The double notes in measures 11-12 require careful fingering to create a *legato* sound. Only beats 2 and 3 in this passage can actually be played with a true finger *legato*. To create a *legato* effect on the other double notes, keep your fingers as close to the keys as possible. Practice this skill in the warm-up below.

- When changing fingers on a repeated-note pattern, bounce slightly from the wrist and aim for the same spot on the key. Practice this skill in the L.H. alone, measures 9-11. Begin slowly, gradually increasing the speed. Think of the eighth notes in groups of four.

Quick Quiz

1. Play the R.H. melody in measures 1-2. Find two variations of this melody in the rest of the etude: measures _____ and _____.

2. A *melodic sequence* is a pattern of notes repeated on different pitches. Find two measures in the R.H. part that contain melodic sequences: measures _____ and _____.

Creative Corner

- Play this etude at an *Adagio* tempo and add the damper pedal. Listen carefully to the chord changes, pedaling as often as necessary to avoid blurring the sound.
- Now play your *Adagio* version in the minor mode (C minor). Let your ear be your guide. The sample measures below will help you get started.

Moderato (♩ = 69/92)

23.

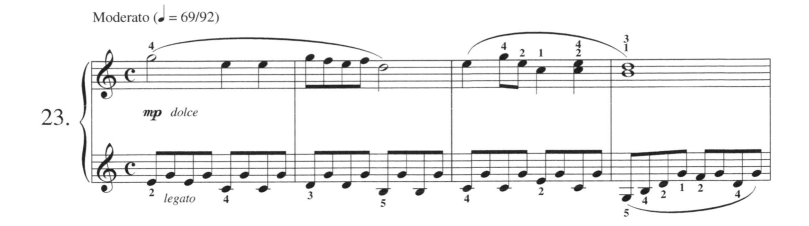

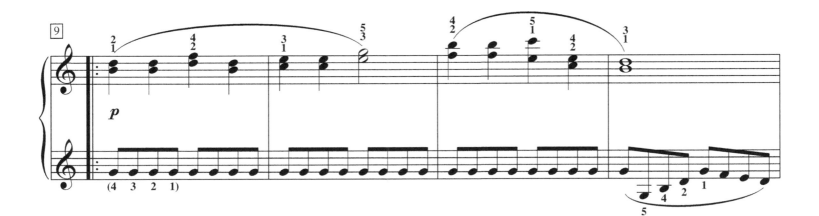

Etude 24

Practice Tips

- In this etude, an *Alberti Bass* pattern appears for the first time in 16th notes.
- When playing *Alberti Bass* in a quick, *Allegro vivace* tempo, keep your fingers close to the keys and play with an even, light touch. Play each L.H. group of four 16ths with a natural pulse on finger 5.
- Keep a good arch, balancing the weight of your arm evenly over all fingers as you play.

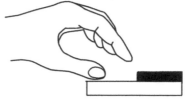

Keep a good arch.

- First practice the L.H. alone, blocking the chords in each measure to become familiar with the harmonic patterns. Then practice the R.H. melody with L.H. blocked chords before playing the etude as written.

- The R.H. melody contains several octave extensions. Play these by 'opening' your hand in a relaxed manner, rather than by stretching out with effort or tension. Let your hand and arm follow your fingers as you extend your hand position to play the higher note.

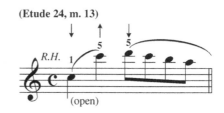

(Etude 24, m. 13)

Quick Quiz

1. Play the L.H. part, measure 1, beats 3-4. What chord is outlined by these four notes? _____
2. Is this chord in root position, first inversion, or second inversion? _____
3. Compare the R.H. part, measures 1-4 to measures 5-8 and measures 13-16. How are these three phrases the same? How are they different?
4. Measures 5-8 and 13-16 are good examples of: *sequence*, *variation*, or *inversion*. _____

Creative Corner

- Create your own melodic variations of measures 1-4 in measures 5-8 and 13-16.
- Transpose this etude to D Major. The key signature contains two sharps (F-sharp and C-sharp), and each note will move up one whole-step. The L.H. chord progression in D Major is outlined below.

(Etude 24)

- Play this etude in its minor mode, C minor. The key signature contains three flats (B-flat, E-flat, and A-flat). However, be sure to play B-natural whenever the **V** or **V7** chord is used.

38

Etudes 25, 26, and 27

Practice Tips – Etude 25

- Playing quick patterns between the hands in this etude presents a rhythmic challenge. For example, in measure 1, the L.H. plays the downbeat and immediately passes the sound to the R.H. 16th notes. The R.H. 16ths must follow the L.H. at once, in one quick impulse. Exactly the reverse is true in measure 17. Practice this quick, precise exchange of notes between the hands in the warm-ups below.

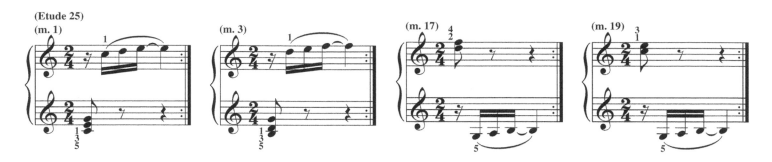

- Apply this practice tip to other measures that have the same rhythm pattern.
- Tuck your thumb under fingers 2 and 3 well in advance on all scale passages so that it is ready to play in time and without a 'bump.' In descending scale passages, bring finger 3 over gently without turning your wrist.

Practice Tips – Etudes 26 and 27

- Focus on shifting smoothly from one R.H. double note to the next. Keep a good arch, and feel the shape of each interval in your hand. Stay close to the surface of the keys as you play, and let your hand and arm follow your fingers.
- Practice the R.H. double-note shifts in *Etude 26*, measures 12-16, in the warm-up below. Repeating each double note in a 'long-short' pattern helps build security and confidence while thinking ahead to the next position.

Apply this practice technique to similar passages in *Etudes 26* and *27*.

Quick Quiz

1. In *Etude 25*:

    What scale is found in measures 1-2? _____

    What scale is found in measures 17-18? _____

    What scale is found in measures 27-28? _____

2. In *Etude 26*:

    What five-finger pattern is found in measure 1? _____

    What five-finger pattern is found in measure 17? _____

Creative Corner

- Create a new L.H. part for *Etude 27*, measures 1-8, using a broken-chord accompaniment based on the original L.H. harmonies. Follow the rhythmic pattern that is found in the L.H., measures 4 and 8.

Allegretto vivace ($\flat$ = 96/$\downarrow$ = 104)

25.

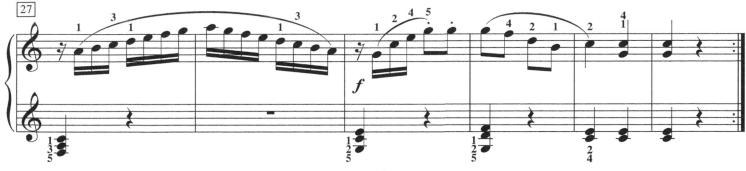

26.

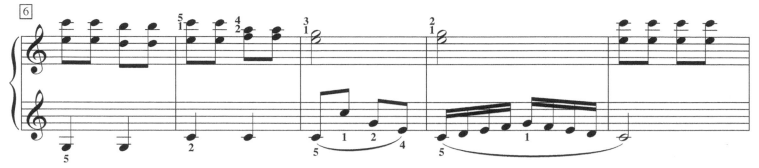

Allegretto (♪ = 104/♩. = 72)

27.

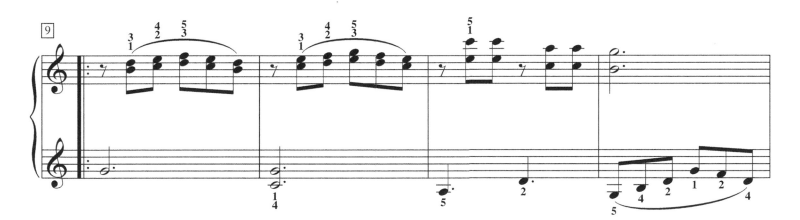

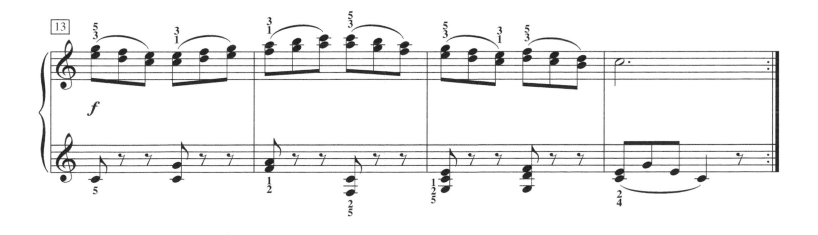

Etudes 28 and 29

Practice Tips – Etude 28

- The type of *Alberti Bass* in this etude is often used in 3/4 time. Balance the weight of your arm and hand over each finger, giving a natural pulse to the first beat of each measure. Keep your fingers close to the surface of the keys as you play. Doing this will help you play the accompaniment as lightly as needed.
- The R.H. melody has both two- and three-note slurs. Use a drop/lift motion of the wrist and hand on each one. In longer phrases, transfer the weight of your hand and arm freely from finger to finger.
- Shape this etude musically, adding *crescendo* and *decrescendo* appropriately.

Practice Tips – Etude 29

- The two-note slurs that begin on a weak beat (beats 3 or 6) and end on a strong beat (beats 1 or 4) need special attention. Use a drop/lift motion of the wrist here, but also give a slight accent to the *second* note of each slur to maintain the correct metric pulse.

(Etude 29, m. 1, 2)

- The repeated notes in measures 10-11 and 14-15 will be easier to play up to tempo if you use alternating fingers, 1-2-1, rather than the thumb only.

Quick Quiz

1. In *Etude 28*, name the R.H. chord and identify it as root position, first inversion, or second inversion in:

    Measures 1-2: _____ _____

    Measures 3-4: _____ _____

    Measures 9-10: _____ _____

2. In *Etude 29*, name the R.H. chord outlined in:

    Measure 11: _____

    Measure 22: _____

Creative Corner

- Create a new L.H. part for *Etude 29* using a waltz-bass pattern. Use the sample measures below as a guide.

(Etude 29, m. 1-3)

- By turning the R.H. melodies upside-down (inverting them) in *Etude 29*, you can create an entirely new melody. Refer to the version written out for you on page 47 as a guide. Experiment with other melodic variations on your own.

Allegretto vivace ($\downarrow$ = 112/160)

28.

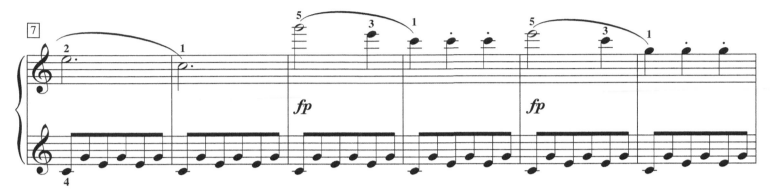

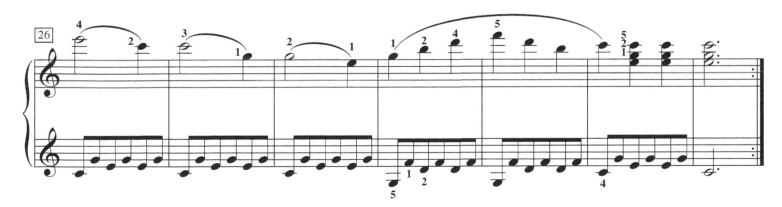

Allegretto vivace (♪ = 116/♩. = 84)

29.

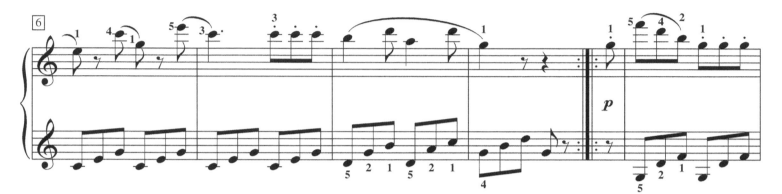

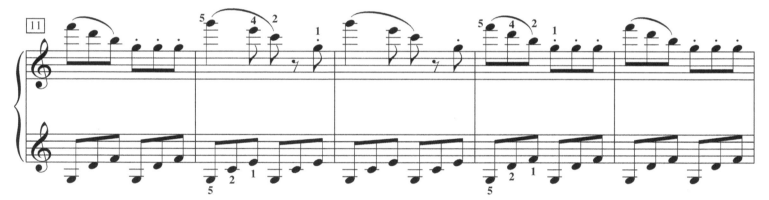

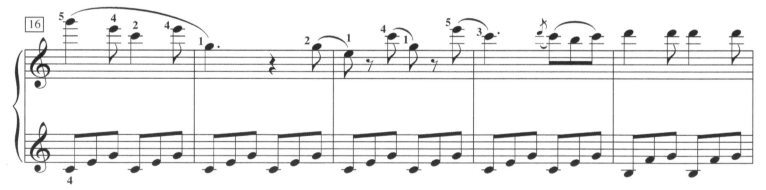

Allegretto vivace (♪ = 116/♩. = 84)

29.
(variant)

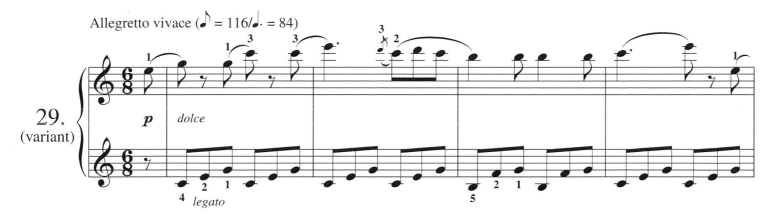

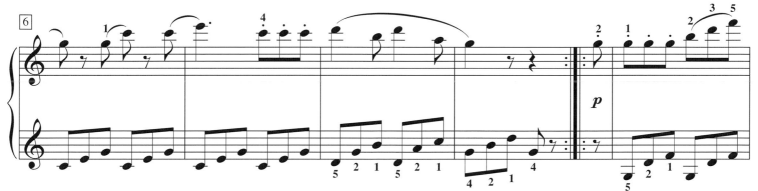

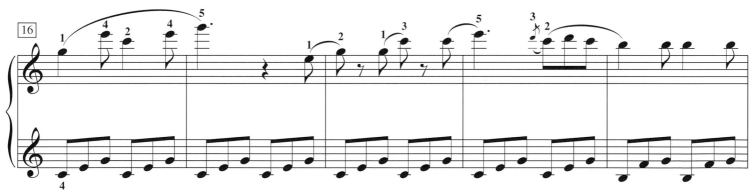

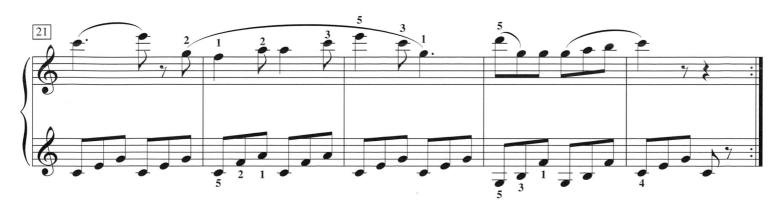

Quick Quiz Answer Key

Page 8: Etudes 1, 2, 3, and 4

1. 6th
2. L.H. measure 6, beat 3
3. They both contain the same note names in all but one measure, but *Etude 3* uses them in quarter notes.
4. C Major

Page 10: Etudes 5, 6, and 7

1. Measures 13-14. The L.H. notes are not the same, making the harmonic progression **I-IV-I** instead of **I-V-I**.
2. Eight (measures 5, 8, 14, 17, 18, 21, 22 and 30)

Page 14: Etudes 8, 9, and 10

1. C Major
2. Measures 7-8, 11, 15, 17-18, 21, 23-24, 27 and 31.
3. F Major
4. Second inversion

Page 18: Etudes 11, 12, and 13

1. G Major
2. 10th; 6th; 6th; 10th

Page 22: Etude 14

1. G Major
2. Second inversion
3. D7
4. D
5. Measure 1: A, C; Measure 9: B

Page 24: Etude 15

1. Two. Measures 1-4 and 9-12; Two. Measures 5-8 and 13-16
2. C Major; first inversion
3. C Major; second inversion

Page 26: Etude 16

I-I-IV-I-I-I-V7-I

Page 28: Etudes 17, 18, and 19

Pattern B

Page 32: Etudes 20, 21, and 22

1. Some choices might be: Clementi, Beethoven, Mozart, Haydn, Latour or Diabelli
2. CM/I-CM/I-GM/V-GM/V-CM/I-CM/I-G7/V7-CM/I

Page 36: Etude 23

1. Measures 5-6 and 13-14
2. Measures 6-7 and 14-15

Page 38: Etude 24

1. F Major
2. Second inversion
3. Lead students to discover details of the melody that make these phrases similar or different.
4. Variation

Page 40: Etudes 25, 26, and 27

1. C Major; G modal; A natural minor
2. C Major; G Major

Page 44: Etudes 28 and 29

1. C Major – second inversion; C Major – first inversion; C Major – root position
2. G7; F Major